The Lord's Prayer

PRAYING WITH POWER

New Community Bible Study Series

JOHN ORTBERG

WITH KEVIN & SHERRY HARNEY

New Community
KNOWING. LOVING. SERVING. CELEBRATING.

The Lord's Prayer

PRAYING WITH POWER

ZONDERVAN.com/
AUTHORTRACKER
follow your favorite authors

The Lord's Prayer: Praying with Power
Copyright © 2008 by Willow Creek Association

Requests for information should be addressed to:

Zondervan, *Grand Rapids, Michigan* 49530

ISBN 978-0-310-28057-6

Interior design by Sherri Hoffman

Printed in the United States of America

10 11 12 13 14 • 21 20 19 18 17 16 15 14 13 12 11 10 9 8 7 6 5 4 3 2

CONTENTS

God has created us for community. This need is built into the very fiber of our being, the DNA of our spirit. As Christians, our deepest desire is to see the truth of God's Word as it influences our relationships with others. We long for a dynamic encounter with God's Word, intimate closeness with his people, and radical transformation of our lives. But how can we accomplish those three difficult tasks?

The New Community Bible Study Series creates a place for all of this to happen. In-depth Bible study, community-building opportunities, and life-changing applications are all built into every session of this small group study guide.

How to Build Community

How do we build a strong, healthy Christian community? The whole concept for this study grows out of a fundamental understanding of Christian community that is dynamic and transformational. We believe that Christians don't simply gather to exchange doctrinal affirmations. Rather, believers are called by God to get into each other's lives. We are family, for better or for worse, and we need to connect with each other.

Community is not built through sitting in the same building and singing the same songs. It is forged in the fires of life. When we know each other deeply—the good, the bad, and the ugly—community is experienced. Community grows when we learn to rejoice with one another, celebrating life. Roots grow deep when we know we are loved by others and are free to extend love to them as well. Finally, community deepens and is built when we commit to serve each other and let others serve us. This process of doing ministry and humbly receiving the ministry of others is critical for healthy community life.

Build Community Through Knowing and Being Known

We all long to know others deeply and to be fully known by them. Although we might run from this level of intimacy at times, we all want to have people in our lives who trust us enough to disclose the deep and tender parts of themselves. In turn, we want to reveal some of our feelings, expressing them freely to people we trust.

The first section of each of these six studies creates a place for deep knowing and being known. Through serious reflection on the truth of Scripture, you will be invited to communicate parts of your heart and life with your small group members. You might even discover yourself opening parts of your heart that you have thus far kept hidden. The Bible study and discussion questions do not encourage surface conversation. The only way to go deep in knowing others and being known by them is to dig deep, and this takes work. Knowing others also takes trust — that you will honor each other and respect each other's confidences.

Build Community Through Celebrating and Being Celebrated

If you have not had a good blush recently, read a short book in the Bible called Song of Songs. It's a record of a bride and groom writing poetic and romantic love letters to each other. They are freely celebrating every conceivable aspect of each other's personality, character, and physical appearance. At one point the groom says, "You have made my heart beat fast with a single glance from your eyes." Song of Songs is a reckless celebration of life, love, and all that is good.

We need to recapture the joy and freedom of celebration. In every session of this study, your group will commit to celebrate together. Although there are many ways to express joy, we will let our expression of celebration come through prayer. In each session you will take time to come before the God of joy and celebrate who he is and what he is doing. You will also have opportunity to celebrate what God is doing in your life and the lives of those who are a part of your small group. You will become a community of affirmation, celebration, and joy through your prayer time together.

You will need to be sensitive during this time of prayer together. Not everyone feels comfortable praying with a group of people. Be aware that each person is starting at a different place in their freedom to pray in a group, so be patient. Seek to promote a warm and welcoming atmosphere where each person can stretch a little and learn what it means to be a community that celebrates with God in the center.

Build Community Through Loving and Being Loved

Unless we are exchanging deeply committed levels of love with a few people, we will die slowly on the inside. This is precisely why so many people feel almost nothing at all. If we don't learn to exchange love with family and friends, we will eventually grow numb and no longer believe love is even a possibility. This is not God's plan. He hungers for us to be loved and to give love to others. As a matter of fact, he wants this for us even more than we want it for ourselves.

Every session in this study will address the area of loving and being loved. You will be challenged, in your personal life and as a small group, to be intentional and consistent about building loving relationships. You will get practical tools and be encouraged to set measurable goals for giving and receiving love.

Build Community Through Serving and Being Served

Community is about serving and humbly allowing others to serve you. The single most stirring example of this is recorded in John 13, where Jesus takes the position of the lowest servant and washes the feet of his followers. He gives them a powerful example and then calls them to follow. Servanthood is at the very core of community. To sustain deep relationships over a long period of time, there must be humility and a willingness to serve each other.

At the close of each session will be a clear challenge to servanthood. As a group, and as individual followers of Christ, you will discover that community is built through serving others. You will also find that your own small group members will grow in their ability to extend service to your life.

Bible Study Basics

To get the most out of this study, you will need to prepare and participate. Here are some guidelines to help you.

Preparing for the Study

1. If possible, even if you are not the leader, look over each session before you meet, read the Bible passages, and answer the questions. The more you are prepared, the more you will gain from the study.
2. Begin your preparation with prayer. Ask God to help you understand the passage and apply it to your life.
3. A good modern translation, such as the New International Version, Today's New International Version, the New American Standard Bible, or the New Revised Standard Version, will give you the most help. Questions in this guide are based on the New International Version.
4. Read and reread the passages. You must know what the passage says before you can understand what it means and how it applies to you.
5. Write your answers in the spaces provided in the study guide. This will help you participate more fully in the discussion and will also help you personalize what you are learning.
6. Keep a Bible dictionary handy to look up unfamiliar words, names, or places.

Participating in the Study

1. Be willing to join in the discussion. The leader of the group will not be lecturing but will encourage people to discuss what they have learned in the passage. Plan to share what God has taught you during your preparation time.
2. Stick to the passages being studied. Base your answers on the verses being discussed rather than on outside authorities such as commentaries or your favorite author or speaker.

3. Try to be sensitive to the other members of the group. Listen attentively when they speak, and be affirming whenever you can. This will encourage more hesistant members of the group to participate.
4. Be careful not to dominate the discussion. By all means participate, but allow others to have equal time.
5. If you are a discussion leader or a participant who wants further insights, you will find additional comments in the Leader's Notes at the back of the book.

The Lord's Prayer: Praying with Power

Imagine you love golf. You buy golf magazines and instructional videos, subscribe to the Golf Channel, and play whenever you can. One day there's a message on your answering machine from Tiger Woods, offering to fly you to Pebble Beach, California, to give you some tips on how to improve your game. He'll spend a weekend golfing with you and personally help you hone your skills.

Do you think you'd take him up on his offer? That's a no-brainer! Of course you'd say yes!

Whatever our area of deepest passion, all of us would jump at the chance to learn from someone who is known as the best. It would be a delight to "sit at that person's feet" and receive instruction from a master.

This same excitement and anticipation should fill our hearts when we think about learning from Jesus himself about how to pray. He was not just a master; he is *the* Master! At the feet of Jesus we can learn to pray with a new depth, passion, and fruitfulness.

I think if you were to ask Jesus' disciples, "What was the secret of Jesus' life? What enabled him to live with such extraordinary joy, clear direction, and amazing wisdom?" I believe they would have answered with one word, "Prayer." No one has ever prayed like Jesus; prayer was the core of his being.

In Luke 3:21–22 we're told that as Jesus prayed during his baptism, the heavens opened and the Holy Spirit came on him. He experienced the Father's pleasure when he heard these words: "You are my Son, whom I love; with you I am well pleased." Then he immediately went into the wilderness for forty days of fasting, solitude, and prayer.

In the busy times of life, when his schedule got demanding, Jesus made space for prayer. Luke writes, "But Jesus often withdrew to lonely places and prayed" (Luke 5:16). A short time later Luke adds this account: "One of those days Jesus went out to a mountainside to pray, and spent the night praying to God. When morning came, he called his disciples to him and chose twelve of them, whom he also designated apostles" (6:12–13). Can you imagine what that night must have been like? Jesus went out into the hills and spent the whole night praying. In the morning he chose those who would be his closest followers. Jesus bathed the big decisions of life in prayer.

Jesus also prayed when he was in pain and grieving. In Matthew 14:3–13 we read that John the Baptist, Jesus' cousin, was executed. When Jesus heard what had happened, he withdrew to a solitary place to be alone with the Father.

Jesus prayed when he was concerned for his friends. Knowing Peter would face a time of great struggle, Jesus said, "Simon, Simon, Satan has asked to sift you as wheat. But I have prayed for you, Simon, that your faith may not fail. And when you have turned back, strengthen your brothers" (Luke 22:31–32). Imagine how Peter must have felt knowing Jesus was praying for him.

Jesus prayed when he faced his ultimate challenge: "Jesus went out as usual to the Mount of Olives, and his disciples followed him. On reaching the place, he said to them, 'Pray that you will not fall into temptation.' He withdrew about a stone's throw beyond them, knelt down and prayed, 'Father, if you are willing, take this cup from me; yet not my will, but yours be done.' An angel from heaven appeared to him and strengthened him. And being in anguish, he prayed more earnestly, and his sweat was like drops of blood falling to the ground" (Luke 22:39–44).

From the beginning to the end of Jesus' ministry, his disciples had a front-row seat to watch the greatest pray-er who ever prayed. And as they watched, they saw him filled with peace, wisdom, spiritual power, and grace. When Jesus prayed, they saw things happen.

This six-week study of the Lord's Prayer gets right down to the heart of life and faith. It looks at our deepest passion and longing . . . to know and experience God.

You and I will probably never get a private golf lesson from Tiger Woods, financial advice from Bill Gates, or cooking classes from Wolfgang Puck. But we have an even better offer. We can learn to pray from Jesus, the world's greatest pray-er ever!

Just like his followers asked him to teach them to pray two thousand years ago, we can make the same request today. I invite you to do exactly that as you begin this study. Quiet your heart and speak to Jesus. Say, "Teach me to pray." This will launch you into an adventure like none other you have ever experienced. "Lord, teach me to pray!" You can be confident that this is a prayer he will answer.

The "Who," "Where," and "What" of Prayer

MATTHEW 6:5–15

Has your mind ever wandered while you were praying? You want to be focused and engaged in the experience, but the next thing you know you are wondering if you remembered to turn off the stove, if you closed the garage door, or if you should take a vacation next summer. A wandering mind is something we all face as we seek to become people of prayer.

Psychologists talk about a condition they call "mindlessness." For some of us, mindlessness is a problem we suffer occasionally in prayer and in life. For others, mindlessness is a way of life. We can be physically present, but our minds are floating off somewhere in space, on autopilot.

Jesus taught that mindlessness is one of the biggest obstacles to prayer. He said, "And when you pray, do not keep on babbling like pagans, for they think they will be heard because of their many words" (Matthew 6:7). Jesus knew that prayer can sometimes deteriorate into mindless babble or "sacred" worrying. We all have experienced this. We begin praying sincerely only to start rambling through a series of words with no idea of what we're saying.

Jesus gave the prayer recorded in Matthew 6:9–13 as a tool to help us get beyond such mindlessness. He intended to give us a simple structure and some helpful themes and categories to focus on so that we could remain mindful as we pray. Sadly, in many church traditions we have made the recitation of this prayer a mindless routine. Week after week we repeat the words but our minds and hearts are not engaged. Jesus was looking for exactly the opposite. He wanted this prayer to become a springboard into the deep, refreshing waters of intimate conversation with the God we love. Indeed, Christians have used it this way for over two thousand years.

When we pray "Our Father," we should be moved to reflect deeply on the person and tender care of God. When we say, "Hallowed be your name," we should be inspired to give him worship, adoration, and praise. If we dare to declare, "Your will be done," we should be propelled into prayers of submission and surrender. As we ask for our "daily bread," we should find ourselves humbly telling God about the needs we have in our lives and in the lives of those we love. Jesus did not give us a prayer to memorize and repeat over and over until our minds go blank. It is a launchpad from which we are lifted to high places of worship, petition, confession, and so much more. Every time we pray this prayer, something new and fresh can happen.

Making the Connection

1. If you grew up reciting the Lord's Prayer in church or your home, how was this prayer used?

If you did not grow up with this prayer, what is your perception of how it is understood and used by Christians?

Knowing and Being Known

Read Matthew 6:5 – 15

2. As you read Matthew 6:9 – 13, what are the "Big Themes" that Jesus is teaching us to focus on as we pray?

-

-

-

-

-

-

Which theme above do you find most natural for you to pray about? How do you enter into prayer about this topic or theme?

3. Which theme in the Lord's Prayer tends to get neglected as you engage in conversations with God?

How do you hope this study will help you go deeper in this area of your prayer life?

The "Who" of Prayer

Have you ever felt guilty about your prayer life? Most of us have. The reason for this low-grade guilt is what I call a "who" problem. We get confused about the nature of the person to whom we are praying. We start to think that God is angry with us or at least a little disappointed. This "who" problem can keep us from growing more passionate, intimate, and effective in prayer.

Jesus begins this prayer with the words, "Our Father." When we begin praying, it is important to stop our hurried minds and acknowledge the fact that we are speaking to someone. God is personal. When Jesus taught his followers to say "Our Father," he introduced the most unique opening line in the history of prayer.

Every time we use a name, we make a statement about the nature of the relationship. That's why names are so powerful. In formal relationships we might say "Mr." or "Mrs." If we are talking to a friend, we usually call them by their first name. If it's a real close friend, sometimes we use a nickname. When we say "Father" or "Daddy," we are expressing that we are in an intimate family relationship.

Read Romans 8:15 – 17 and Galatians 4:6 – 7

4. When Jesus invited us to address God as "Father" he understood that none of us have perfect earthly fathers. If we think of our heavenly Father as being a cosmic version of our earthly father, we will have a confused prayer life (no matter how good or bad our earthly father has been). Instead, Jesus is teaching us that we have a perfect, loving, and powerful Father in heaven. What kinds of things would a great earthly father do for his children?

What sorts of things does our Father in heaven want to do for his children?

5. Some people don't like the idea of addressing God as "Father." What might we lose if we do away with calling God our Father?

6. How have you experienced God's fatherly love, protection, or provision?

The "Where" of Prayer

Jesus teaches us to pray to "Our Father in heaven." How far away is heaven? We tend to think of heaven as someplace in outer space. As a result we can imagine that God is remote, distant, and hard to access.

To correct this misconception it helps to know a little background on the grammar of the phrase "Our Father in heaven." The Greek word for heaven is *uranos*, from which we get the word for our planet Uranus. In the Lord's Prayer, it is the plural form of the word. Literally the prayer is, "Our Father, the one in the heavens." This phrase is used a variety of ways in the New Testament: for the atmosphere, for the sky, and also for the air we breathe.

(cont.)

It is this final sense of the word that Jesus intends in this prayer. When you pray, "Our Father who is in the heavens," you are saying, "Our Father who is all around me," "Our Father who is closer than the air I breathe," "Our Father who is right here, right now." God is that close! We are never alone.

7. What makes us feel that God is far away and that there is a great distance between us and him?

8. How have you experienced God's nearness and presence in your life?

9. If God were sitting in a chair right in front of you, what would you ask him? What would you tell him?

How might your prayer life change if you knew God was sitting beside you, ready to hear what is on your heart?

The "What" of Prayer

Most of us have times when we are not exactly sure what we ought to pray about. This "what" problem can get in our way. We're not sure what God might be interested in. Does he really care about the little stuff of life? Is he all that interested in the things that matter to me? The truth is that there is no concern, no matter how small, that God does not care about. There is no request, no matter how silly or trivial it may seem, that God doesn't want to hear. He wants us to talk with him about everything, even our daily bread. God cares about the little things and the big things of life.

However, at this point I want to note the very first request included in the Lord's Prayer is, "Hallowed be your name." A name in the Bible is never just a label. It's a reflection of the person, his or her character and identity. We are to "hallow" or give the honor that is due to the name of God. To God himself! We are to praise, revere, and exalt the name of God.

Read Exodus 20:7 and Psalm 66:1 – 4

10. Why do you think God is so concerned that his name not be misused?

What are some of the ways the name of God is abused and misused, and how can we seek to honor his name in a world that tends to trample on it?

11. Throughout the Bible there are many names for God. What is a name for God that you love and what does this name express about God's character and nature?

Celebrating and Being Celebrated

Take time as a group to pray, using the Lord's Prayer to guide you. First, recite the prayer in unison together. Here are some guidelines for this reading:

Rule #1: Read in monotone without any hint of emotion.

Rule #2: Keep your mind vacant. Don't actually think about what you're reading. Pretend you are reading numbers from the phone book.

Rule #3: Whatever you do, don't be the first one to start reading a new line. Nobody else might join you and you'll be speaking all alone.

No ... don't actually use these rules! Read the Lord's Prayer together with minds that are engaged, hearts that are open, and lips that are expressing some of the most beautiful words ever spoken.

"Our Father in heaven,
hallowed be your name,
your kingdom come,
your will be done
   on earth as it is in heaven.
Give us today our daily bread.
Forgive us our debts,
   as we also have forgiven our debtors.
And lead us not into temptation,
   but deliver us from the evil one." (Matthew 6:9–13)

Next, have someone read each line of the Lord's Prayer and then offer up brief prayers that grow naturally out of that portion of the prayer:

Read: Our Father in heaven, hallowed be your name,
Prayers . . .

Read: your kingdom come, your will be done on earth as it is in heaven.
Prayers . . .

Read: Give us today our daily bread.
Prayers . . .

Read: Forgive us our debts, as we also have forgiven our debtors.
Prayers . . .

Read: And lead us not into temptation, but deliver us from the evil one.
Prayers . . .

Loving and Being Loved

In our human relationships we express love through our bodies. We give hugs and kisses. We smile. We give a wink or a nod to say "I love you and you matter to me." In a very similar way we can express love to God through our body language. In particular, our posture in prayer can be a way to communicate love to the God who loves us without reservation.

What posture do you use when you pray? What do you do with your eyes? What do you do with your body? How do you use your hands?

Some people have grown up in a tradition where they heard, "Every head bowed, every eye closed," when it was time to pray. This might feel like a hard and fast biblical rule, but the truth is, the Bible never tells us to close our eyes and fold our hands. These are things we teach children so they won't get distracted or poke other kids during prayertime.

According to the Bible, Jesus' common posture for prayer was "he stood and looked into the heavens." Scripture also records, among other stances, people praying as they knelt, as they lay prostrate on the ground, as they sat with their hands stretched out, and with faces lifted toward the sky or bowed down toward the earth. The point is that there is not an exact posture of prayer, but we should engage our bodies in our expression of prayer.

Experiment this week with different physical expressions as you pray. Find something that feels right as you do your best to express love to the God who calls you his child.

Serving and Being Served

If you have children, grandchildren, nieces, nephews, or young people you can influence, consider teaching them to pray the Lord's Prayer. Don't just help them memorize the words and repeat them over and over. Teach them to use this great prayer as a springboard into deep and refreshing places of conversation with God.

Your Kingdom Come

MATTHEW 6:10

Ken Davis recounts a story from the days when Mike Ditka was coaching the Chicago Bears football team. Davis writes:

One day Ditka was about to deliver a locker room pep talk and he looked up and saw defensive tackle William "Refrigerator" Perry. Then again, how could he NOT see him? At 338 pounds the Fridge stood out even in a crowd of pro football players! Ditka gestured to the Fridge and said, "When I get finished I'd like you to close with the Lord's Prayer." Then the coach began his talk.

Meanwhile, Jim McMahon, the brash and outspoken quarterback, punched John Cassis and whispered, "Look at Perry, he doesn't know the Lord's Prayer." Sure enough Perry sat with a look of panic on his face, his head in his hands, sweating profusely. Cassis replied, "Nah ... sure he does! He's just nervous. Everybody knows the Lord's Prayer!" After a few minutes of watching the Refrigerator leak several gallons of sweat, McMahon nudged Cassis again and said, "I'll bet you 50 bucks Fridge doesn't know the Lord's Prayer."

When Coach Ditka finished his pep talk, he asked all the men to remove their caps. Then he nodded at Perry and bowed his head. The room was quiet for a few moments before the Fridge began to speak in a shaky voice and said, "Now I lay me down to sleep. I pray the Lord, my soul to keep ..."

Cassis felt a tap on his shoulder. It was Jim McMahon who whispered to him, "You win. Here's the 50 dollars. I had no idea Perry knew the Lord's Prayer."

People are not born knowing the Lord's Prayer. And those who learn it often fail to really understand the depth and significance of what they are praying. One line of the prayer that seems to be the least understood of all is, "Your kingdom come, your will be done on earth as it is in heaven" (Matthew 6:10). Most Christians do not have a great deal of clarity on what the kingdom of heaven is. There's a good reason for this. We can barely understand what this earth would look like if God's kingdom were to really break into human history. It boggles the mind.

One technical phrase that's often used to define the kingdom of God is the "range of God's effective will." Imagine everything that God desires to happen actually happening—the time, place, and reality when all he desires is what we experience. That's God's kingdom.

Making the Connection

1. If God's kingdom were to break fully into human history while you sleep tonight, what is one thing that would be different when you wake up tomorrow morning?

Knowing and Being Known

Read Matthew 6:9 – 15

2. What is something you know God desires for this world in *one* of the following areas:
    • In marriages
    • In families
    • In your nation
    • In the life of the local church

3. Followers of Christ are called to pray for God's will to be done. We are also expected to do our part to help bring about kingdom transformation in our world. Considering the items listed in question two, what is one action you could take to be part of God's plan to bring his kingdom to this earth?

4. As you think about the life and ministry of Jesus, what were some of the signs that the kingdom of God was breaking into human history?

The Kingdom Is Near ... The Kingdom Is Here

Jesus lifted up the message of God's kingdom over and over. It was core of his gospel. In Mark we read, "After John was put in prison, Jesus went into Galilee, proclaiming the good news of God. 'The time has come,' he said. 'The kingdom of God is near. Repent and believe the good news!'" (Mark 1:14–15). When Jesus says the kingdom of God is near, he's not saying it's getting kind of close. He's saying it's available now. It has broken into human history ... it's here!

In human history, there is only one life that has been lived in which God's will had total unhindered sway. Jesus bore in his own person, in his flesh and blood, the reality of the kingdom of God. Everybody who saw him saw a life lived in the reality of God, a life in which whatever God desired became reality. But the story does not end there. Jesus lets his followers know that it is now possible for human beings to live in the presence and power of God. We can do it right now. The kingdom is near ... the kingdom is here. We can live a life saturated with the presence and power of God, we really can.

5. Though there is turmoil and trouble in the world today, God is still on the move and his kingdom is near and here. As you look at your life, your church, other followers of Jesus you know, and the work of God around the world, what are some of the signs you see that assure you that God's kingdom is near and here?

Kingdoms in Conflict

It would be glorious if only one kingdom were at work in this world. But that is simply not the case. There was Caesar's kingdom in Jesus' day, and there are many political and economic kingdoms today, all exercising power and flexing their muscles, seeking to have influence over us. Besides these, there are entertainment kingdoms, athletic kingdoms, educational kingdoms, and the list goes on. And, of course, spiritual forces also are at work in the heavenly realms, trying to keep us from walking in the power of God's kingdom. If we are going to be successful in praying for God's kingdom to come and walking in the power of his kingdom, we must be ready to resist the lures of other false kingdoms.

God's kingdom is near and here, but one day it will come in all its fullness. One day there will be no other kingdoms. There will come a time when every other kingdom will be swept away and we will experience God's rule and authority unleashed in all its glory. What a day that will be!

Read Daniel 2:29 – 45

6. This passage in Daniel is one of many in the Bible that bring the same powerful and hope-filled message about God and his kingdom. How does this particular passage bring hope for those of us who are praying for God's kingdom to come and his will to be done?

7. How do you see the kingdoms of this world at war with the values and vision of God's kingdom?

How can we resist and fight against the influence of the world's kingdoms as we pray for God's kingdom to come?

Becoming Kingdom Pray-ers

How will God's kingdom come to earth? Amazingly, it all starts with prayer. This is why Jesus calls us to cry out, "Your kingdom come." Jesus asks you and me to be kingdom pray-ers. We do this as we pray in three distinct directions.

First, pray that the kingdom of God will break into your life and invade your soul. Pray that God would have full rule in every area of your life; hold nothing back. This could become the most powerful, dangerous, and transformational prayer you ever lift up. Next, pray for God's kingdom power and presence to be unleashed in the church and among other believers. It must begin among God's people, his followers. Then, pray for an in-breaking of the kingdom of God in our world. Pray that false kingdoms will fall and that the rule of God will sweep through political structures, economic systems, and all other human kingdoms.

Read 2 Corinthians 10:3 – 6 and Ephesians 6:10 – 18

8. What are some specific ways you can pray for each of the following:
   - For the kingdom of God to break into your life on every level

   - For God's kingdom to be unleashed and realized in power in the life of the local church

   - For the kingdom to come in culture and society

9. Every society has kingdoms and spiritual strongholds that resist the kingdom of God. What are some of the little or big kingdoms in your community and society that God wants you to pray against?

What actions might you add to your prayers in an effort to see these kingdoms fall and the kingdom of God come?

Becoming Kingdom Bearers

When we dare to boldly pray, "Your kingdom come, your will be done," we are declaring to heaven and earth, "I'm ready to suffer for the cause of Jesus. I'm ready to endure whatever it takes to help usher in God's kingdom. I am ready to take up the cross and enter the spiritual battle that is already raging." This prayer goes beyond just the battle, but it is certainly part of what we are expressing.

We are also declaring, "God, may I become the kind of person who does your will from my heart. May your kingdom come to earth in my life. May I be a kingdom bearer." When we become kingdom pray-ers the next logical step is that we are transformed into kingdom bearers. We begin to dream about and experience what it looks like when the kingdom of God begins to break into our lives — into our workplaces, families, relationships, financial choices, motives, and even our dreams. When we become kingdom bearers, everything changes.

Read Matthew 16:24 – 26

10. What are some of the consequences and costs you might face if you become a consistent kingdom pray-er and bearer?

11. What is one way you can be a kingdom bearer in a specific area of your life in the coming week?

How can your group members pray for you and cheer you on as you seek to bear the kingdom of God in this area of your life?

Celebrating and Being Celebrated

We have the amazing privilege of being kingdom pray-ers. In question eight you discussed some specific ways you can pray for God's kingdom to come. Use your group reflections to lead you in a time of prayer for the in-breaking of the kingdom of God in your lives, your church, and our world.

Loving and Being Loved

One important aspect of bearing the kingdom of God into the world is reaching out to people who are far from God. Identify at least one person God has placed in your life who is spiritually disconnected. Commit to pray for God's kingdom to invade and break into his or her life. Also, pray for opportunities to bear the presence and power of Jesus in your life as you interact with this person.

Serving and Being Served

Get a map of your area and begin praying for God's kingdom to come and his will to be done in each town. Pray for cities, communities, and neighborhoods by name. You might want to post this map where you will see it on a regular basis and use it as a prayer prompter.

Daily Bread

MATTHEW 6:11

Jesus taught us to pray, "Give us today our daily bread."

You can picture it, and so can I. A sixteen-year-old girl stands at her open closet door packed from floor to ceiling with shirts, pants, dresses, shoes, sweaters, coats, and all kinds of other clothes. Her eyes scan back and forth, up and down. She pushes clothes on hangers left and right, looking for something … anything that suits her fancy. Her face is locked in an expression bordering somewhere between disappointment and disgust. Then she says it. While standing in front of a wall of clothes that could dress a medium-sized village of people, she cries out, "I don't have anything to wear!"

Jesus taught us to pray, "Give us today our daily bread."

A thirteen-year-old boy spends five minutes rummaging through the kitchen cupboards and refrigerator looking for a snack. He scans the six kinds of cereal lined up in colorful boxes. He passes over two kinds of toaster pastries because the fruity filling (with little actual fruit) is not his favorite. He snarls in disgust at the half-dozen beverage options because someone else has finished his favorite flavor of soda and has dared to leave the empty bottle in the fridge just to taunt him. At last he shouts at the top of his lungs, so his parents, the neighbors, and all of heaven can hear, "There's nothing to eat in this house!"

Jesus taught us to pray, "Give us today our daily bread."

It is painful to watch a teenager complain about "nothing to wear" or "nothing to eat," when they, for most of them, actually have more than enough. Sadly, this attitude does not seem to go away as we grow past adolescence into adulthood. In some cases, it only gets worse. We can find ourselves comparing what we have to those around us, only adding to the feeling that we don't have enough.

How do we learn to pray for daily bread when eight-year-olds carry around cell phones that cost as much as a family's full-year income in many parts of the world? What does it mean to ask God for enough bread for the day when we live in a meat-and-potato world? What does this portion of the Lord's Prayer say to those living in a time of abundance and plenty?

Making the Connection

1. Give an example of a person (yourself or someone else) who expressed the feeling that they did not have enough, but in reality, they had so much.

How do you think God feels when his children stand at a full closet or refrigerator and complain that they need more?

Knowing and Being Known

Read Matthew 6:11

The Power of Perspective

One of the best ways to understand what it means to pray for, and live with, daily bread is to relate closely with people who really do need a loaf of bread (or pot of beans or pan of rice) for the new day. If they don't have it, they will be in desperate straits.

(cont.)

Many churches have made a commitment to take adults and students on mission trips or plunge experiences. These "perspective-giving" adventures allow people to come face to face with poverty and pain they might not see in their normal day. After returning from a mission trip to the Dominican Republic or a remote place in Africa, people are changed. After serving a Thanksgiving meal to people who are living on the streets, they gain new perspective. These poignant moments are transformational and radically affect our attitudes and lifestyles ... for a week or two!

Sadly, a brief foray into the inner city or another country often impacts us for only a short time. Then we resume life as usual. What we need to learn is how to daily adjust our perspective so we are consistently aware of how much we really do have.

2. Describe a moment when you experienced a perspective shift and realized how much you have compared to many people in the world who have very little.

3. What can we do to keep a healthy perspective on material things? How can we, on a daily basis, maintain an attitude that we have daily bread and much more?

The Countercultural Call to Contentment

Contentment, in many circles, is equivalent to being lazy, unmotivated, and even unpatriotic! In a culture where upgrading your computer, car, and clothing are considered normal and desirable behavior, contentment is the enemy. Most of us are predisposed to want more and more. Then, when we get what we were dreaming about, we often want even more.

Into our pathologically greedy world, Jesus teaches, "Pray for what you need ... for your daily bread." Such an idea begins to make sense only when we seek to live with contentment. This is the discipline of simplicity, the process of learning to say one powerful word, "Enough!" As we learn to enjoy what we have and not always strive for more, contentment grows in our hearts. As that happens, our daily bread starts to look like what we really need. And it even tastes better.

Read 1 Timothy 6:6 – 10 and Philippians 4:10 – 13

4. What does the apostle Paul warn about being discontent and always wanting more?

How is contentment presented in a positive light in these passages?

5. Name some mind-sets and attitudes in our culture that push us away from living a truly contented life.

6. Take a moment and write down some of the material things God has provided for you:
   - Where you live ...

   - Your transportation ...

   - Toys and fun stuff ...

   - Tools and things that help you do your work ...

   - Furniture and appliances ...

   - Other things ...

Think of daily bread representing the basics of life, what you really need (not all of your wants). How might your life change or look different if you experienced inner contentment?

Authentic Thankfulness

Parents say it over and over and over through the childhood years as they raise their little boy or girl. "What do you say?" they ask. They are looking for a very specific answer, just two little words: "Thank you!" Of course, they also want their son or daughter to really mean it. But, for now, just hearing it would be a good start.

God has given his children daily bread and, in many cases, so much more. When we learn to say "Thank you," he is delighted. One of the ways we can honor God is by praying for our daily bread and actually thanking God when we get it. Think about the parent who has asked their child, "What do you say?" countless times over the years. Then, one day, their daughter just says it. "Thank you!" She was not coaxed or prodded, and Dad or Mom can tell by the look in her eyes that she really means it. What a day that is for a parent! In the same way, God waits for his children to come to a place of authentic and natural thanks.

Read James 1:16 – 18; Ephesians 5:19 – 20; and Psalm 100

7. Why is thankfulness so important in the life of a follower of Jesus?

What do we declare to God and the world when we live with authentic thankfulness for our daily bread?

8. How has God provided daily bread (or more) for you? Share your thankfulness to God with your group members.

Sharing Our Bread

Jesus did not teach us to pray, "Give *me* today *my* daily bread." He said to pray for *our* daily bread. He wants us to be concerned not only about what *I* need, but what *we* need. All through the Bible we see that God's heart beats for those in need. If we see with the eyes of God, feel with his heart, and serve with his hands, we will also care about those who have no daily bread. We will actually be willing to joyfully share the bread we have with those who have none.

Read 1 John 3:16 – 18; Matthew 25:31 – 36; and Luke 12:32 – 34

9. How have you experienced the sharing of daily bread accomplishing *one* of the following:
   - Reminding you that all of your bread is a gift from God
   - Showing others in God's family that they are loved and that he wants to provide for them
   - Revealing to spiritual seekers that God's compassion and love is alive in the hearts of his followers

10. What are some ways the local church can engage more intentionally in sharing daily bread with people in your community?

11. What one specific way could you take another step forward in sharing your daily bread with people in need?

Celebrating and Being Celebrated

In question six you listed some of the things God has provided for you. Take time as a group to offer prayers of thanks for God's loving supply of daily bread and so much more.

Loving and Being Loved

Often we try to protect young people from the harsh realities of this world. If we have plenty of daily bread, we are afraid to let them see, with their own eyes, people who struggle each day just to survive. Consider taking a child, a niece, a nephew, or even a class of young people from your church to serve at a local mission or shelter. You will need to contact the organization first to make sure they are ready for your visit.

Use this as a springboard to talk about things like:
- How much we have
- The real needs in the world

- What it means to have "nothing to eat" or "nothing to wear"
- How we can share our bread with others
- Other questions that come up

Serving and Being Served

If you want to create a regular opportunity to share your daily bread and have your perspective adjusted, consider supporting a child through World Vision or another relief agency. Keep a picture of this child on your refrigerator or even on your dining room table. Pray for them at meals. Read about their home country and how they live. If you have children or grandchildren, invite them to be part of this ministry by providing them a giving jar in which they can deposit donations.

Forgive Us Our Debts

MATTHEW 6:12, 14–15; 18:21–35

Jesus taught us to pray, "Forgive us our debts, as we also have forgiven our debtors." What does it mean to *be* a debtor? What does it mean to *have* debtors? What is Jesus asking us to pray?

Maybe the simplest way to explain this is in the arena of finances. Let's say that you have borrowed money to buy a house and a car and have used a credit card to pay for gasoline, groceries, and clothing. Who is expected to pay the monthly mortgage or payment? The basic rule of society can be summed up quite clearly: You owe … you pay! It is a rare thing indeed to have someone else offer to pay off your debt. You are a debtor, and the bank wants their money.

If you are not sure how this rule works, feel free to test it out. Go to your bank and ask to chat with a bank officer. Express your feelings honestly: "This debt that I carry is just too much for me. It's hampering my lifestyle. It is hard to pay these bills every month. In fact, paying back the money I owe you is getting a bit depressing. So, I think I'll quit. Are you comfortable with my choice?"

You'll likely discover that people who lend money are quite touchy about the whole "paying it back" thing. They keep very careful accounts of what is owed to their institution. If you fail to pay back a bank, you will learn that they have a whole team of people ready to help you realize the importance of repaying your debt. If you borrow from a less reputable institution, they sometimes have people on the payroll who will make a personal visit and do whatever it takes to get the money you owe. There is an aquatic animal metaphor for a person who loans money and collects by using strong measures. We call that person not a guppy, a goldfish, or a clown fish … but a loan *shark*. They know the rule: You owe … you pay.

In this prayer, Jesus is addressing another kind of debt. It is the debt of sin and moral failure. The truth is, each one of us has a mountain of moral debt we can't pay off. It is a debt against God and other people. We also know that others have sinned against us and they can't pay their debt either. Each one of us has been the perpetrator of sin and the victim of sin. We have debtors and we are debtors.

As Jesus teaches us to pray, he calls us to ask God to forgive us as we forgive others. Charles Williams wrote, "No word in English carries a greater possibility of terror than the little word 'as' in that clause." Why? Because Jesus makes a correlation between the way I treat my debtors and the way God Almighty will treat me as a debtor.

Making the Connection

1. How have you experienced the rule "You owe ... you pay" in your financial life or in some other area of life?

Knowing and Being Known

Read Matthew 6:12, 14 – 15 and 18:21 – 35

2. Both these passages have a surprisingly harsh edge when it comes to the idea of forgiving others the way God has forgiven us. According to them, what is the connection between God's forgiveness toward us and the way we forgive others?

What kind of responses and emotions arise when you read these passages?

3. Imagine you are one of the characters in the Matthew 18 parable. From your perspective, what happened in the story and what should a reader of this parable learn? (Try to give your response in the first person ... as you believe that person would have responded.)
    - The king

    - The servant who was forgiven a great debt

    - That same servant who would not forgive a small amount

    - The other servants who stood at a distance and watched the drama unfold

You Owe ... You Pay

The parable in Matthew 18 seems to grow from a real-life situation. It appears that Peter has a debtor; someone has wronged him. Knowing that Jesus is big on the whole forgiveness thing, Peter asks if he should forgive up to seven times. This was over twice as many times as the rabbis would normally recommend. Jesus' response was staggering. He said we should forgive seventy-seven times (or seven times seventy). The point was that there should be no end to our forgiveness.

In the parable, the normal human system of economics (and forgiveness) is presented clearly. The servant owed a great debt and the time of payment came due. Because he could not pay his debt, he would face consequences and they would be severe. This would not surprise Jesus' listeners because they knew the rule: You owe ... you pay. The servant had a debt that was insanely large (bigger than the gross national product of the kingdom). He could not pay it. So, off to jail with him and his whole family.

Read Matthew 18:21 – 25

4. How would the king in the parable have been justified in doing all he could to get some of his money back from this man?

5. The king in the parable is a picture of God. Our sin against a perfect and holy God has created a debt bigger than we can imagine or dream. How would God be justified and fair if he decided to enforce the "You owe ... you pay" rule?

You Owe ... I Pay

The king in the parable is moved with compassion. Looking at the frightened, selfish, desperate, foolish servant, he's moved with pity. He does two things, and in the original text he does them in this order. First, he releases the man and his family — no prison, no torture, no forced labor ... he lets him go. Next, he does the unthinkable; he forgives the debt. He wipes it away. First he removes the punishment and next he removes the debt.

The king forgives a mountain of debt, a huge sum of money. And the debt doesn't just disappear. Somebody has to pay, and it's the king himself. He offers a whole new system of debt management: You owe ... I'll pay. This is the economy of grace. The king says, "I will pay the unpayable debt. I will take the hit. I will suffer the loss. I will take the whole price on myself so you can go free. You owe ... I'll pay."

This is really a story about the human race. This is our story. Jesus says there is a king, there is a God, who is lavishly generous and painstakingly just. Human beings have accumulated a mountain of unpayable moral debt because of our sins. But the king comes and says, "You owe ... I'll pay." It cost him the life of his beloved Son. It cost him the best he had, and he paid it without hesitation." That is grace. That is debt-canceling at its best.

Read Matthew 18:26 – 27 and Colossians 2:13 – 15

6. How does the cross of Jesus act as the ultimate debt repayment in human history?

Take a moment and think about your mountain of moral debt that Jesus canceled through his sacrifice on the cross. How are you like the forgiven servant in this story?

7. In light of all that followers of Jesus have been forgiven, how should we treat people who have sinned against us (our debtors)?

You Owe ... I Won't Forgive

In act two of this parable, the freshly forgiven and newly debt-free servant encounters a man who owes him some money. The debt is really just lunch money compared to the millions he has been forgiven. The debtor pleads for patience and time to pay him back.

Jesus' listeners would expect the radically forgiven servant to extend the same grace and debt-erasing plan to a fellow servant. Instead, the story takes a bizarre twist. The man who had been forgiven a king's ransom refused to forgive someone else the lunch money they owed. Imagine the shock of Jesus' listeners to learn that the man who was saved by grace showed no compassion. He actually grabbed the debtor by the throat in a gesture of violence and contempt, and demanded to be paid back. This recipient of an ocean of grace would not offer a thimble of forgiveness to someone else!

Read Matthew 18:28 – 30

8. At this point in Jesus' story, what kind of feelings and emotions do you think he was seeking to evoke in the hearts of his listeners?

9. What are some examples of how we can be just like the unforgiving servant in this story?

How do you think God feels about people who have been forgiven
all of their sins and yet still refuse to extend grace to others?

Read Matthew 6:12, 14–15 and 18:31–35

10. Even when we know this story and the spiritual truth being
    communicated, it is still hard to forgive. What keeps us from
    forgiving others a comparatively small debt, even when we
    know God has forgiven us an infinitely larger debt?

He Paid ... I Must Forgive

The final act in the drama of this parable is painful to watch. We discover that this is a tragedy. The first servant is brought before the king, but this time there are no tears, no pleadings, and no bargains. The king says to the slave (a loose paraphrase), "You didn't get it at all, did you? It didn't penetrate. You have badly misunderstood me, my friend. You thought grace meant I was a fuzzy-minded incompetent and that I would let you get away with whatever you wanted and abuse whomever you chose. You used my grace as an excuse to be the same old, hurtful, self-centered, unforgiving person you were before. You were shown forgiveness, but you won't give it. You were granted mercy, but you won't bestow it. You were showered with love, but you won't extend it at all. You were offered the economy of grace, and you've chosen the economy of vengeance. Have it your way."

This moment in the parable unveils a sobering reality. When we know that God has paid the price for all of our sins through Jesus Christ, we are expected to live in his debtor-forgiveness plan. It is no longer a moment-by-moment choice. It is now an expectation. He paid ... I must forgive.

---

11. Without using names, share a personal story about *one* of the following:
- How you extended grace and forgiveness to someone, living in God's debt-reduction plan
- A time when you did not forgive someone else and how this impacted you, your relationship with God, or your relationship with others
- A situation where someone refused to forgive you and the consequences of this unforgiveness

Celebrating and Being Celebrated

Take time as a group to read the following passages. You might want to invite group members to volunteer to read the passages.
- 1 Corinthians 15:3
- 2 Corinthians 5:16–21
- Colossians 2:13–15
- 1 Peter 3:18
- Revelation 1:4–6

Spend time in prayer celebrating the gift Jesus offered when he died on the cross in your place to cancel the debt of your sins.

Loving and Being Loved

God's ultimate act of love was a sacrifice. He paid a price so that he could extend forgiveness to his lost, broken, and undeserving children. We are called to be part of this same debt-reduction plan. Make a list of people you have not yet been able to forgive (their debt against you could be small or quite large). Then, begin to ask God for the strength, courage, and awareness of his grace that is needed to extend forgiveness. One by one, take the life-giving step of forgiving each individual.

Serving and Being Served

Ephesians 4:15 says:

> Instead, speaking the truth in love, we will in all things grow up into him who is the Head, that is, Christ.

Because the call of Jesus to forgive is so clear and because the consequences of ignoring this call are so severe, we are propelled forward on our journey of forgiveness. At the same time, we can invite others along. When we encounter followers of Jesus who say things like, "I will never forgive him," or "I don't think I will ever be able to forgive what she did to me," we should be prepared to speak the truth in love. The business of forgiveness is for everyone who follows Jesus. It should mark our lives. The world should look on in awe! Be bold in sharing this critical and often neglected calling with others. As you do, it will help you to be more intentional about growing as one who forgives your debtors.

Deliver Us from the Evil One

MATTHEW 6:13; I CORINTHIANS 10:6–13

We were having dinner at the home of friends. It was a beautiful evening so we were eating outside. Every so often I'd hear a strange sound, a kind of electric "zap." Finally my curiosity got the best of me and I asked, "What's that zapping sound?" "Oh, it's the sound of bugs hitting our bug zapper," they said, and went on to describe the gadget that attracted insects with its light, only to sizzle them when they got too close. It went on all night long—bug after bug—hundreds of bugs. "Zap! Zap! Zap!"

I must admit that this experience got me trying to think like a bug. You'd think that an approaching bug might observe the tray underneath the zapping light filled with hundreds of dead bugs and wonder, "Is this a good idea?"

Only a bug could possibly be that dense, right? Only a bug would go flying mindlessly into the same trap that countless other bugs have died in, right? Well, let's think about the glowing light of temptation that the Evil One places in front of human beings. Listen closely and you will hear it. Political leaders. "Zap!" Pastors and church leaders. "Zap!" Successful business leaders. "Zap!" Wealthy athletes. "Zap!" Homemakers. "Zap!" Construction workers, televangelists, school teachers. "Zap! Zap! Zap!" It never seems to end.

Ever since Eve saw that the fruit of the tree was good for food and pleasing to the eye and desirable for wisdom, "Zap!" Over and over we read and hear of people who fall into temptations that devastate their lives, destroy their marriages, rock their worlds, break up their families, and wither their souls. Why do we voluntarily give in to what we know is going to be destructive? Why do we fly into the light?

The Bible teaches that we have an enemy who is bigger, stronger, and smarter than us. He is devoting time, investing energy, and marshaling the forces of hell in an effort to draw us into sin. This is why the Bible is filled with warnings about the Evil One:

> Finally, be strong in the Lord and in his mighty power. Put on the full armor of God so that you can take your stand against the devil's schemes. For our struggle is not against flesh and blood, but against the rulers, against the authorities, against the powers of this dark world and against the spiritual forces of evil in the heavenly realms. (Ephesians 6:10–12)

> Be self-controlled and alert. Your enemy the devil prowls around like a roaring lion looking for someone to devour. (1 Peter 5:8)

> "You belong to your father, the devil, and you want to carry out your father's desire. He was a murderer from the beginning, not holding to the truth, for there is no truth in him. When he lies, he speaks his native language, for he is a liar and the father of lies." (John 8:44)

> "And lead us not into temptation, but deliver us from the evil one." (Matthew 6:13)

Making the Connection

1. Imagine you are a military commander expected to brief the troops on the enemy they will be fighting ... Satan. What would you tell them about the tactics he uses to lure people into sin?

Knowing and Being Known

Read I Corinthians 10:6 – 13

Three Keys in the Battle Against Temptation

First Corinthians 10:6 – 13 is a synopsis of the sins into which the people of Israel were lured while they wandered the desert for forty years following their escape from Egypt. Some of these sins were repeated over and over again: idolatry, immorality, testing God, grumbling. After this brief history of one of Israel's low points, the apostle Paul identifies three truths to give hope and encouragement to those facing temptation.

1. *Temptation will come to everyone ... expect it.* This is not meant to discourage us; just the opposite. We are not alone. Every follower of Jesus will face temptation. Even Jesus was tempted (Matthew 4:1 – 11). Of course, he did not give in and commit sin. But if the Evil One tried to tempt Jesus himself, we had better believe he will come after us as well. When we let this truth sink into our hearts and lives, we will be ever vigilant and watching out for places the enemy might seek to attack. This preparedness becomes a weapon to resist the devil.

2. *God will not let us be tempted beyond what we can handle.* There is no temptation we will face that is not first filtered through the Father's eyes and caring hands. God is faithful and will not allow the enemy to tempt us beyond our ability to resist. This truth brings hope but it is also sobering. We can never rationalize our sin by saying, "I couldn't help myself. I just couldn't resist any further." God knows what we can handle and will never allow us to be tempted beyond what we can stand against ... in his power.

3. *God will provide a way of escape.* When temptation comes, we need to look around. There is always a way out. We might have to run or we might have to fight. It could be a big "No!" or the exercise of Spirit-led self-control, but there is always a way out.

2. How does each of the truths in 1 Corinthians 10:13 bring hope and strength to followers of Jesus when we are facing temptation?

3. What is one area of temptation you are facing in your life today and what are some possible "ways out" that God has provided?

The Strength of Joy

In the rest of this session we will be looking at three specific actions that we can take to find a way out of temptation and the cycle of sin. If I had to name the single greatest emotional resource against temptation in one word, it would be the word *joy*. The first way out of temptation is to arrange your life around joy. Set up your life so that you can experience high levels of the joy of the Lord.

What we often forget is that joylessness is always a setup for vulnerability to sin and disobedience. One writer puts it like this: "Failure to attain a deeply satisfying life always has the effect of making sinful actions seem good." Our success in overcoming temptation will be easier if we are joy-filled.

Read Nehemiah 8:10

4. How could joy in *one* of the following areas act as a deterrent to temptation:
    - In the workplace
    - In your marriage
    - In how you use your resources
    - In your family life
    - In how you serve among God's people

5. What actions, decisions, and lifestyle choices have you found that help to unleash lasting joy in your heart?

6. What are the big joy-busters that tend to come in and drive you toward joylessness?

    What can you do to avoid these joy-stealing situations?

The Wisdom of Accountability

The second way out of temptation that God provides is developing relationships of accountability. Temptation always involves keeping things hidden in the darkness. When we humbly tell trusted friends about our areas of struggle with sin, a light begins to shine and the power of sin begins to die. The enemy wants us to keep our sins, struggles, and temptations in the dark and to ourselves. He wants us to say in the quiet of our heart, "I can handle this on my own. I don't need to tell anyone else about this. It would be better if no one ever knew about my sin." The problem is, we have an enemy who is stronger and smarter than we are. Thankfully, God is infinitely stronger and smarter than the Evil One. If we try to fight on our own, we are bound to lose. We need to invite God and God's people into the process.

Read James 5:16

7. What are some of Satan's lies and deceptions that make us fearful to tell others about our temptations and sins?

   What are some legitimate reasons people are apprehensive about sharing the dark places of their sin and temptation?

8. How can we press past the lies and the legitimate concerns and move to a place of authentic and faith-strengthening accountability?

The Sword of the Spirit

Another way out of temptation God offers is the power of the Bible. There is amazing strength in knowing and following the Word of God. When the tempter came to Jesus at the beginning of his ministry (see Matthew 4; Luke 4), the weapon Jesus used over and over was the truth of Scripture. Once, twice, three times the Evil One tempted him. Each time Jesus countered by quoting the Bible, "It is written." Jesus' mind was so washed in the Word, and he lived in its reality so thoroughly, that he saw right through Satan's deceptions.

Too often we consider memorizing verses or sections of the Bible as an exercise for children so they can get a gold star on a chart. Jesus saw the Word of God as a powerful weapon against the enticements of the devil. Like a sword, he could wield this weapon with great effectiveness. If we are in a spiritual battle—and we are—then it is time for us to sharpen the sword and get ready to fight back.

Read Matthew 4:1 – 11; Hebrews 4:12; and Ephesians 6:17

9. What do you learn from Jesus' use of Scripture, and how can you emulate his battle tactics?

10. Describe a time when you faced temptation and Scripture became your weapon to resist the enticements of the enemy.

11. What personal disciplines can you put in place to help you dig deeply into the Bible and meditate on the truth of God's Word?

If you want your small group, or a member of the group, to keep you accountable in developing this discipline, invite them to do so.

Celebrating and Being Celebrated

In this session we have looked honestly and soberly at the reality that the devil is a formidable enemy. But we also have been reminded that God's power in us is far greater than the influence of the enemy. Reflect on the passages below and spend time as a group celebrating the power and victory we have in Jesus:

You, dear children, are from God and have overcome them, because the one who is in you is greater than the one who is in the world. (1 John 4:4)

And I saw an angel coming down out of heaven, having the key to the Abyss and holding in his hand a great chain. He seized the dragon, that ancient serpent, who is the devil, or Satan, and bound him for a thousand years. (Revelation 20:1–2)

Submit yourselves, then, to God. Resist the devil, and he will flee from you. Come near to God and he will come near to you. (James 4:7–8)

Loving and Being Loved

Joy is one of the "ways out" that God provides when we are facing temptation. Take time in prayer to ask God to help you identify someone in your life who is lacking joy. Commit to finding a way to be a joy-bearer in their life. As you seek to bring joy to this person, pray that it will fortify them to resist temptation and remain faithful to God's call on their life.

Serving and Being Served

One of the best gifts you can give to another follower of Jesus is to be a person of such character that they can trust you to keep them accountable. Take time to reflect on how trustworthy you are. Are you able to keep confidences? Will you pray faithfully? Will you be a partner at their side as they engage in spiritual warfare? When you feel you are ready, offer yourself as an accountability partner to a close Christian friend.

Yours Is the Kingdom and the Power and the Glory

MATTHEW 6:9–13

Human beings have a kingdom problem. We think, "Everything is about my kingdom, my power, and my glory." One of the best commentaries I know on this complex topic is a book on political science theory by a theologian named Dr. Seuss. The book is called *Yurtle the Turtle*. My parents read it to me when I was growing up, and I read it to my children.

It's a story about a little pond filled with little turtles who were ruled, or so he thinks, by a king named Yurtle. One day Yurtle the turtle king decides that his kingdom needs extending. "I'm king," he said, "of all I see. But I don't see enough. That's the trouble with me." So he began to stack turtles up to make himself a turtle throne.

The king lifts his finger and a whole pond of turtles scramble to obey, first dozens and then hundreds. They all exist for his sake, his kingdom, his power, and his glory. Atop his throne at last, he can see for miles. "I am Yurtle the turtle, oh marvelous me, for I am the ruler of all that I see."

Yurtle thinks his throne is as secure as a throne could be. And I suppose in a way it was. But in the end, his throne turns out to be a turtle tower of Babel. "And the turtle on the bottom did a plain little thing. He burped. And that burp shook the throne of the king. And today that great Yurtle, that marvelous he, is king of the mud. That's all he can see." This is how self-made thrones always end up. They can be human thrones, turtle thrones, or any kind of throne. If it is not the throne of God, it will always collapse and end up in the mud.

Jesus said, "So the last will be first, and the first will be last," and, "For whoever exalts himself will be humbled, and whoever humbles himself will be exalted" (Matthew 20:16; 23:12). This is biblical truth. It's just the way things are in God's kingdom. We are wise to learn this lesson and commit ourselves to God's kingdom, power, and glory. We can try to build our own kingdoms, stack some turtles, and put ourselves first, but Jesus invites us to a life focused on his kingdom, his power, and his glory.

Making the Connection

1. What are some of the "turtle thrones" we build to exalt ourselves and make us look bigger than we really are?

What are some of the little "burps" that can cause these human thrones to come tumbling down?

Knowing and Being Known

Read the Lord's Prayer as printed below and on page 63:
Our Father in heaven,
hallowed be your name,
your kingdom come,
your will be done
    on earth as it is in heaven.

Give us today our daily bread.
Forgive us our debts,
    as we also have forgiven our debtors.
And lead us not into temptation,
but deliver us from the evil one.

For yours is the kingdom and the power and the glory forever. Amen.

Yours Is the Kingdom

Like it or not, we are little kingdom builders. We want to make our families, work, friends, and sometimes even our churches into little kingdoms under our control. We want life to be about our agendas, our wants, and our needs. Some people are bold and obvious about this and others are stealthy and subtle. But we all have the same problem.

Jesus is inviting us to recognize, every day, that another kingdom is at work in this world that may not be as visible or look as impressive to human eyes or seem as urgent. But it is the most important kingdom of all. We may wonder from time to time whether God's kingdom is going to be the last kingdom standing, but it will be. So we pray, "Your kingdom, not my kingdom." In these words we express humble surrender.

---

2. When you get involved in "personal kingdom" building projects, how can this impact *one* of the following areas of your life:
    - Your vocation
    - Your friendships
    - Your relationship with God
    - Your marriage or parenting
    - Your use of personal resources
    - Some other aspect of your life

3. What have you discovered that helps you keep your mind, heart, and energy focused on God's kingdom building projects and off of personal kingdom pursuits?

Yours Is the Power

When we rely on our power, we always come up short. When we pray, "Yours is the power," we discover that God can supply all we need. It seems upside-down but this is how things work in God's kingdom. Ask yourself a few questions: Do I need power in my life? Do I face challenges at work I can't seem to manage? Are there places and situations in this world I am concerned about? Do I lack the strength needed to restore and heal a broken relationship? Do I have a friend or family member who needs power beyond what they can muster? Do I struggle with worry, fear, or concerns that keep me up at night? If you said yes to any of these questions, the answer is *not* to try harder. It is *not* to pull yourself up by your spiritual bootstraps. The answer is to admit, "I can't do it. I lack the power to make these things right." When we come to this point, we can cry out, "Yours is the power," and things will begin to turn around.

Read Acts 12:1 – 11, 18 – 19, 21 – 24

4. This account in Acts captures an epic example of how human power and God's power are radically different. What do you learn about human power in this passage and what do you learn about God's power?

5. We all face situations in this life in which we lack the power and strength to make it through on our own. Tell about when you faced a situation like this, cried out for God's power, and he brought you through.

   How do you think this situation would have turned out if you had insisted on pressing forward in your own strength?

6. Where do you need God's sustaining power today?

   How can your group members pray for you, encourage you, and even be conduits of God's power as you face this situation?

Yours Is the Glory

It is possible to cry out, "Yours is the kingdom! Yours is the power! And mine is the glory!" When God's kingdom is breaking into our lives and when his power is flowing, the Evil One will entice us to take the credit and try to get the glory. We must battle this temptation toward pride and self-glorification. The antidote is passionate worship. When we are on our knees in prayer, lifting up our voices in worship, or pointing to God and declaring, "To God be the glory," it is hard to be consumed with pride.

Read Psalms 34:1 – 3; 63:3 – 4; and 86:12 – 13

7. When we are humbly honest, only God deserves to be glorified and lifted up in worship. What are some reasons that God deserves glory (and we do not)?

    God Is: **We Are:**

    •   •

    •   •

    •   •

    •   •

8. It is easy to give God glory and praise when we gather for worship services with other Christ followers. But if we are going to live a "Yours is the glory" lifestyle, it will mean worshiping God all through the week. What are some of the ways you keep your heart, lips, and mind filled with worship in the flow of an ordinary day?

Every Knee Will Bow

In our world, God's name is not always hallowed. Countless times every day the name of God is used by one human being to curse another; so too is the name of Jesus thrown around and treated in profane ways. But one day the true King will lift his finger, and a whole lot of thrones that seem real secure will come tumbling down. A whole lot of big turtles are going to end up flipped over on their backs ... stuck in the mud with their little feet waving in the air. The Bible tells us that a time will come when "every knee will bow."

How many knees will bow? Every knee! Try to picture the scene. All humanity, every person from Adam until the very end of time, will bow in acknowledgment of the supremacy of Jesus. Every president who ever lived, every king and queen, every CEO, every movie star, every billionaire … everyone will bow down. Even those who refused to bow the knee in life: Hitler, Stalin, Caesar Augustus, Herod … every knee will bow!

Read Philippians 2:1 – 11

9. How do you see both the humility and glory of Jesus in this passage?

10. One way we bow our knees to Jesus in this life is by humbly following his will revealed in the Bible. In this passage the apostle Paul gives a number of exhortations:
    • Be like-minded, having the same love, being one in spirit and purpose (a call to unity).
    • Do nothing out of selfish ambition or vain conceit (a call to examine our motives).
    • In humility consider others better than yourselves (a call to humility).
    • Look not only to your own interests, but also to the interests of others (a call to service).
    How might you bow your knee in this life by following *one* of the exhortations listed above? Consider at least one practical action.

Celebrating and Being Celebrated

Take time as a group to lift up prayers of celebration in three ways:

- We celebrate your kingdom as it breaks into this world ...
- We rejoice in your power! We need it; unleash it in our lives ...
- We declare your glory! We bow our knees, lift our voices, and give you praise ...

Loving and Being Loved

Take time in the coming week to meet with God on your knees. A day will come when every knee will bow, even those who refused to do so in this life. Meet with God on your knees and declare your love, your devotion, and your commitment to bend the knee regularly and willingly as his follower.

Serving and Being Served

His is the glory! Commit, in a fresh new way, to be a passionate worshiper both in your private life and when you gather with God's family. Purpose in your heart that you will give God praise and glory. Commit to him that you will not just show up for worship, but you will engage yourself fully. Let this be your act of service to the God to whom you say, "Yours is the kingdom and the power and the glory."

Session One – The "Who," "Where," and "What" of Prayer
MATTHEW 6:5–15

Questions 1–3

I think one of the greatest sentences written in the twentieth century was penned by Dallas Willard in *The Divine Conspiracy* when he wrote, "Jesus' intent was to bring his apprentices to the point where they dearly love and constantly delight in that heavenly Father made real to earth in Jesus, and are quite certain there is no catch, no limit to the goodness of his intentions or his power to carry them out." Jesus' design is to bring his friends, you and me, to the place where we dearly love and constantly delight in God.

This is why the Lord's Prayer is so helpful. When we get past the pedestrian uses of the prayer as a routine recitation in church services, we discover that the themes of this prayer capture our imaginations and hearts. This prayer gives shape and form to our thoughts when mindlessness tries to invade.

Questions 4–6

The Old Testament records people using the image of a father to describe God. But there is no record of anyone ever coming to God in prayer and addressing him as Father until Jesus did. Jesus even used the Aramaic word *Abba*. It's not exactly like our word "daddy" because it was an adult word as well as a child's word, but its meaning is very tender and intimate nonetheless.

Jesus not only used this intimate name for God, but he invites us to use it too. That's unbelievable! We are not approaching a distant deity with fear in our hearts. Rather, we come confidently as we approach our "Father," our "Dad," our "Papa."

When some people pray, their first thoughts are: "I haven't prayed enough." "I feel guilty over the prayerlessness of my life." "I'm not sure this will do any good." "I'm not sure I have enough time to do it adequately or know how to do it right." Those thoughts are from the Evil One, designed to keep you from prayer. You must discipline yourself to not allow such thoughts to occupy your mind; set them aside and start with the name "Father."

When we come to God as Father, his heart says, "This is my son. This is my daughter. I love it when you call me Father. I love it when you set aside time to speak with me about whatever is on your heart."

Questions 7–9

Some years ago I reached a point in my life when I was very frustrated with my lack of growth in prayer. So I prayed for almost a year, "Lord, teach me to pray," and one of the things that happened was that someone came into my life who helped teach me more about prayer.

One thing this person said was, "Tomorrow, instead of whatever you would normally do for prayer, take a half an hour and go do what you love and invite Jesus to go with you." So I went and walked along the ocean. You know what? I just prayed involuntarily. As I walked on the beach I found myself saying, "Jesus, look at that water." And, of course, he was already looking at it, so it was nothing new to him. The point is that prayer became a normal expression of communication in a real relationship. I began to experience God with me, in the normal rhythm of my life.

When we begin to understand that God is with us, as close as the air we breathe, some of the old language begins to sound strange. There used to be times, at the beginning of a worship service, when someone would say, "God, today as we come into your presence. . . ." Now that seems strange to me. I imagine God saying, "Where do you think you've been?" "I am with you always," Jesus said, "to the ends of the earth." In a similar way, I remember people praying, "Lord, come and join us, show up in this place, come Jesus." The issue is not God coming to us; it is us recognizing that he is already here!

Questions 10–11

I love stories. Some years ago I heard one that captured this idea of value. I don't know if it actually happened. But this is the story:

An antiques expert stopped by an antique store filled mostly with junk, and noticed on the floor a cat drinking milk out of a saucer. Recognizing that the saucer was actually a vase from China's Ming dynasty — worth a fortune — he thought, *This is the opportunity of a lifetime. The owner obviously doesn't realize what he's got here.*

He went to the owner and said, "That's quite a remarkable cat you have. I'll give you a hundred dollars for it." And the owner said, "Well, the cat isn't really worth anything, and we're kind of attached to it." But the antiques expert persisted.

At last the owner said, "All right." The man handed over a crisp hundred dollar bill and picked up the cat. Then, trying to make it sound like a casual afterthought, he said, "I'll need a bowl or something to feed my new cat. I'll give you another ten bucks for that old saucer." "Oh, I could never do that," the owner replied. "That's actually a piece from the Ming dynasty in China and it's worth a fortune. But it's the strangest thing. Ever since I started putting milk in it, I've sold seventeen cats."

All of us, especially in financial terms, are used to attaching value to things. Sometimes we'll see something of great worth, but appropriate value hasn't been attached to it — people don't seem to recognize what it is worth. This is supremely true of God. We live in a world where his name gets blasphemed and profaned, spoken casually at best millions of times every day all around the globe. It is time for God's people to ascribe to God the worth he deserves. And that's why Jesus says, "Make the first request in your prayer, 'Hallowed be your name.'"

There are many names of God throughout Scripture that we can use to hallow his name. Here are a few to get you started: I AM (Exodus 3:14); Anointed One (Psalm 2:2); Wonderful Counselor, Mighty God, Everlasting Father, Prince of Peace (Isaiah 9:6); Redeemer, Holy One of Israel (Isaiah 41:14); Son of God (Luke 1:35); Savior (Luke 1:47); Lamb of God (John 1:29); Light of the World (John 8:12); and King of Kings and Lord of Lords (Revelation 19:16).

Session Two – Your Kingdom Come
MATTHEW 6:10

Questions 1–3

The writers of Scripture spent an enormous amount of time reflecting on what the earth would look like if it were aligned rightly with the kingdom of heaven. They wrote often about it both in the Old and New Testaments but, because this involves a deep spiritual reality, it is hard to describe. And we are so finite and fallen that we can't fully embrace its glory and goodness. But we can get glimpses, grasp pictures, get a taste.

When we talk about God's kingdom coming into this world, we also use word pictures that can't fully capture the fullness of God's power and presence. But our dream of what could happen will reflect the same vision God reveals in the Bible. As the kingdom comes, marriages become healthy, parents love their children, the poor are fed, justice reigns in the halls of power, the church aches with passion for the lost and broken, and countless other signs of God's grace explode in our lives and culture. What a vision! No wonder Jesus calls us to pray for God's kingdom to come.

Questions 4–5

What would it look like if God's kingdom came, if his will were done on earth as it is in heaven? The Bible talks about this relative to different spheres of human life.

First of all, there's the sphere of *economics and human need.* John writes in Revelation 7:16 that when God's kingdom is fully realized, never again will people hunger and never again will they thirst. Think about what that would look like — the elimination of hunger. No more pictures of little children with swollen bellies. No mothers trying to scrounge around for enough food so that their babies can survive another day. It's not just the end of poverty but the advent of abundance. Amos wrote, "'The days are coming,' declares the LORD, 'when the reaper will be overtaken by the plowman and the planter by the one treading grapes. New wine will drip from the mountains and flow from all the hills'" (Amos 9:13).

Then there's the sphere of *politics,* which in our history is mostly the story of human conflict. Isaiah 2:4 says, "[God] will judge between the nations and will settle disputes for many peoples. They will beat their swords into plowshares and their spears into pruning hooks. Nation will not take up sword against nation, nor will they train for war anymore." Just think about these words—no more fighting, no more hatred. And Isaiah 11:6 says this about the coming world of peace: "The wolf will live with the lamb, the leopard will lie down with the goat, the calf and the lion and the yearling together; and a little child will lead them."

The kingdom imagery continues in Revelation 21, where John describes his vision of the city of God, whose streets are paved with pure gold and which is surrounded by twelve gates, each made of a single pearl. The kingdom of God, John says through pictures, will be a place where the human hunger for beauty is finally satisfied. No more pollution, no more rundown inner city buildings marred by graffiti and broken windows. No more concrete ghettos or barrios.

Maybe the most beautiful words of all about the kingdom are found in Revelation 21:3–4: "And I heard a loud voice from the throne saying, 'Now the dwelling of God is with men, and he will live with them. They will be his people, and God himself will be with them and be their God. He will wipe every tear from their eyes. There will be no more death or mourning or crying or pain, for the old order of things has passed away.'" No more Kleenex and no more funeral homes.

Every day we will be home with God, never separated by sin. In Ezekiel 36:26–28 God promises, "I will give you a new heart and put a new spirit in you; I will remove from you your heart of stone and give you a heart of flesh. And I will put my Spirit in you and move you to follow my decrees and be careful to keep my laws. You will live in the land I gave your forefathers; you will be my people, and I will be your God." No more cold, stony, stubborn hearts. We will never say something that we will regret later. We will never do anything to be ashamed of. We will never do anything to feel guilty about.

We will look into the face of God, and he will be our God, and we will be his people. Every thought will be a prayer, and every prayer will be a conversation with God. The Lord himself will wipe every tear from our eyes. There will be joy inexpressible. What a vision! What inspiration to pray for the coming of the kingdom!

Questions 6–7

How will God's kingdom come and the kingdoms of the earth crumble and fall? How will this broken world get straightened out? People have been trying to make this happen based on human power for a long time. Revolutions come and revolutions go. Governments get overthrown, but still people go on hating each other. Wars still break out. The human heart is still hard as stone. Even the best efforts of churches and well-meaning people have not ended the oppressive presence of false kingdoms.

Sometimes people think if we're just clever enough about economic growth, a rising tide will lift all boats. It hasn't yet. Sometimes people think it's a political deal. Oddly enough, even in the church people think, *If only we could get a certain person elected.* So far the kingdom has not arrived under a national banner.

It will happen as followers of Jesus pray. As we allow the kingdom to break into our lives, day by day. It will come as God, in his sovereign power, continues to enter our world and brings his kingdom with him.

Questions 8–11

Kingdom pray-ers dare to pray: "All right, God, your will be done in my life. Your will be done, not mine, with my children, my marriage, my friendships, my career. And may I bring the reality of your kingdom into my relationships. God, make me a kingdom kind of servant and a kingdom kind of encourager and a kingdom kind of confronter and a kingdom kind of friend."

What might happen if we prayed, "God, your kingdom come, your will be done in my financial life"? It might involve very serious sacrifice. What if we really asked for the kingdom to come in our workplaces, our neighborhoods, every part of our lives?

As followers of Jesus boldly pray like this, action is inevitable. The Holy Spirit of God begins to transform our desires, dreams, and goals. We move naturally from being kingdom pray-ers to being kingdom bearers. We lift up the banner of Jesus and we press on, though the battle rages around us. We take up the cross every day, we deny ourselves, and we follow Jesus. When the people of God love this way ... look out. The kingdom is near ... it is here!

Session Three – Daily Bread
MATTHEW 6:11

Questions 2–3

In Jesus' time it was very common for people to live day to day. Countless workers would wait in the markets and other key places of the city or village in hopes someone would come by to hire them for one day. At the end of that day they would receive their day's pay. If they were not hired on a particular day, no bread for the day! And so, all those who listened to Jesus tell the parable recorded in Matthew 20:1–16 knew exactly what he was talking about.

Interestingly, there are still places in the world today populated by day laborers. These are people who could easily pray, "Give us today our daily bread," and be asking for enough income to feed their families for the next twenty-four hours.

Not all those in your group are at the same place financially. This study is written as if most of the participants *do* have provision of daily bread, because most will. But some may be in a time of dire need — in survival mode — and the topic of the study might hit very close to home. Be sensitive to that fact.

Questions 4–6

Contentment was a radical concept in Jesus' day and it will be in any day. But we live in a time when the accumulation of stuff has taken on monster-like proportions. The mammon that Jesus warned about is so prevalent in most modern societies that we have a hard time even noticing that we have become materialistic.

When someone today says, "I'm quite happy with my home; I don't need a larger one," some people will see this as a bad thing. If a couple decides to downgrade and simplify their life by selling off some of their assets and moving into a smaller, more modest house, friends and family might worry that something is very wrong. If a child tells her parents, "I don't want all the new, expensive designer clothes. I prefer some basic clothes that will wear well for a long time," it might just send her parents to the Yellow Pages looking for the number of a good counselor in town.

Contentment is not the norm. But the Bible says it should be. There is great freedom and peace when we learn to be content with our daily bread.

Questions 7–8

God delights in the thanks of his children. Like a loving parent, he wants us to learn to be thankful. It is almost an art form. When we are thankful, many things happen.

First, our heart changes. We begin to notice all we have and how good God has been. We are no longer fixated on what we don't have, what we want, or our latest obsession. Instead, we get wrapped up in the joy of thankfulness.

Second, our relationship with God grows. Our thankfulness brings joy to God's heart. As we express it, our prayer life expands. As thankfulness flows consistently and freely from our lips, God is exalted!

Third, other followers of Jesus are inspired. Too many people who name Jesus as Savior are still wrapped up in the mindless pursuit of more. When others see a thankful spirit in us and hear our acknowledgment that the bread we have today is from God and it is enough, they can be encouraged to be more thankful.

Fourth, a watching world stands amazed. When we become thankful, truly thankful, this becomes a testimony to the world. Of all people, Christians should be thankful. When we express that thankfulness honestly and enthusiastically, a world that is hungering and searching for something that satisfies will sit up and take notice.

Questions 10–11

All through the Bible we read of God's heartfelt concern for those in dire need, verses such as:

> Do not take advantage of a widow or an orphan.
> If you do and they cry out to me, I will certainly
> hear their cry. (Exodus 22:22–23)

Defend the cause of the weak and fatherless;
maintain the rights of the poor and oppressed.
(Psalm 82:3)

"The Spirit of the Lord is on me, because he has
anointed me to preach good news to the poor. He
has sent me to proclaim freedom for the prison-
ers and recovery of sight for the blind, to release
the oppressed, to proclaim the year of the Lord's
favor." (Luke 4:18–19; see also Isaiah 61:1–2)

For the Lord your God is God of gods and Lord
of lords, the great God, mighty and awesome, who
shows no partiality and accepts no bribes. He defends
the cause of the fatherless and the widow, and loves
the alien, giving him food and clothing. And you are
to love those who are aliens, for you yourselves were
aliens in Egypt. (Deuteronomy 10:17–19)

If God's heart beats for the needy, and he calls us to enter into
his ministry to the world, how can we not make a commitment
to share our daily bread?

Session Four — Forgive Us Our Debts
MATTHEW 6:12, 14–15; 18:21–35

Questions 1–3

We have all been sinned against. We all have sinned against
others.

There are people whom you thought you could trust but they
hurt you. They were jealous or said bad things; they twisted the
truth. Somebody in business deliberately cheated you and took
advantage of you financially. They didn't care that it would break
your heart. Somebody in your own family wounded you. A parent belittled you, neglected you, or withheld affection when you
needed it. A spouse left or betrayed you. A friend attacked you.
We all *have* debtors.

In the same way, we have wronged others. We have sinned
against God and every single person we love. We all *are* debtors.

As we listen to Jesus teaching us to pray and telling the parable of the unforgiving servant, the best thing we can do is look in the mirror. This is the story of our sin and the greatness of God's grace. It is a call to each of us to live grace-filled lives.

Questions 4–5

One talent in Jesus' day was a vast sum of money. In a whole year, all the taxes collected in Judea and Samaria to be sent to Rome added up to only six hundred talents. According to the parable, the servant owed ten thousand talents, so Jesus simply took the highest number in use and made it plural. It's a little like when we say "a zillion dollars." It's a number too high to calculate. It is a number like the national debt.

At this point in the story, several things would be very clear to Jesus' listeners. First, they would wonder how a slave could come into possession of such riches. Kings in those days (and at any time in history) were not in the habit of giving national-debt-size loans to slaves. They would have been struck by the fact that this king was a man of staggering generosity.

Second, they would have wondered what kind of slave would take so much money from a king, blow the whole wad, and make no provision for the day of reckoning. This is a character of unbelievable folly and selfishness.

Third, Jesus' listeners would have taken note that the king of lavish provision was also the king of the settled account, committed to justice. This is not a story about getting off the hook because of vague bookkeeping. This is not the kind of king who would say at the end of the day, "You did the best you could with what you had. We'll let it go."

Matthew, the gospel writer, understood settled accounts. He was a tax collector before he became a follower of Jesus. His whole life had been about settling accounts. Interestingly, this parable is found only in Matthew's gospel. None of the other three includes it.

Questions 6–7

Sometimes we forget that we really are debtors before God. Our sin has piled up to the highest heaven … even if we don't want to acknowledge it. Any time we are less than honest. Every time we fudge an expense account or tax return. Every time we are impatient and unloving with a five-year-old. Every time we should not have made a cutting remark, but did. Every time we should have spoken in love, but didn't. Every time God gave us a gift and we weren't grateful. Every time we gossiped. Every selfish act, every racist joke, every sexually impure thought or deed, every judgmental attitude has become part of our mountain of moral debt. Only the cross of Jesus and only his shed blood are enough to wipe away our sins.

Questions 8–9

I wonder from the way Jesus told this story if the first servant ever really got what grace is about. If you'll notice, the servant never asked for grace in the first place. He asked for the "works" plan. He said to the king, "I will pay for everything. I can take care of the debt myself. I'm good for it." He never asked for grace; he just wanted off the hook. And when grace was given, there was no response, no expression of thanks, no brokenness, no desire to make right whatever he could.

There is a world of difference between wanting to be forgiven and just getting out of trouble. When you want to be forgiven, you want to rebuild a relationship. You want to repent. You want to set things right with the one you offend, because that's part of reconciliation.

But it's painfully clear from Jesus' story that the first servant had no intention of giving grace. He was saved by the king's grace, but he wouldn't offer it in return. What he did not realize was that refusing to extend grace always has big consequences.

Walter Wink writes about a couple named Grossmeyer on a peace-making mission to Poland some years after World War II. While there, they asked a group of Polish Christians, "Would you be willing to meet with some Christians from West Germany? They want to ask for forgiveness for what Germany did during the war and begin a new relationship."

There was a long silence.

Then one of the Polish Christians said, "What you ask is impossible. Every stone of Warsaw is soaked with Polish blood that they spilled. We cannot forgive." The Grossmeyers understood their emotion. They finished the conversation but, before leaving, decided to close the meeting with the Lord's Prayer.

Everyone in the room knelt down together and prayed as Christians have in every country, through every century, for two thousand years. Coming to the words, "Forgive us our debts, as we also have forgiven our debtors," the Polish Christians stopped, unable to continue. Then the same person who minutes before said he couldn't forgive confessed, "I can no longer say this prayer or call myself a Christian if I don't forgive. Humanly speaking, I can't do it. But God will give us the strength." Eighteen months later a group of Polish Christians and a group of West German Christians met in Vienna and established a friendship that lasted a lifetime.

Questions 10–11

To forgive someone does not mean we excuse or tolerate wrongdoing. It doesn't mean always doing what the other person wants us to do. It doesn't mean putting up with meanness, abuse, or neglect. Forgiving does not mean allowing a sinful pattern in someone else's life to go on unchecked and unfettered. It may not even mean reconciling with someone. There is a difference between forgiving somebody and reconciling with them. If somebody sins against us and refuses to acknowledge the truth and repent, we may not be able to reconcile. Reconciliation requires the willingness of both parties.

Forgiving means we give up the right to hurt someone back. We wish them well before God. We actually pray for them to be changed and come to a place of a wholeness with God. We no longer hold hatred in our hearts toward them. Instead, we become so profoundly aware of God's grace in our lives, rich and undeserved, that we must extend it to others.

Session Five – Deliver Us from the Evil One
MATTHEW 6:13; I CORINTHIANS 10:6–13

Questions 1–3

We should never be surprised when we face temptation. Jesus himself was tempted. It's part of being human, and Jesus was fully human. He was also fully divine. When we realize Jesus faced temptation, it becomes clear that nobody is temptation-free. This means that our ability to resist temptation is enormously important.

The core idea of temptation is allowing oneself to be torn away from the God who loves us. In our day, the word "temptation" is often trivialized, reduced to the lure of fattening desserts or petty indulgences. In the Bible, temptation is never trivial. What is at stake is the human soul.

The tempter is not stupid. He's not going to say, "Choose death." He's not going to try to tempt you with something that is obviously destructive and repugnant to you. The most dangerous temptation you face is probably not the most dramatic, but one most likely to subtly lure you away from intimacy with God.

The Evil One doesn't just tempt you to do what's wrong. He tempts you not to do what's right. He wants to keep you from going deep with God. For some people, the greatest temptation is busyness—anything that keeps us from deep prayer, deep love for God, deep trusting faith. For others, the biggest temptation might be the La-Z-Boy and a television set—whatever keeps us from focusing on things of eternal value. When we look for the places the enemy might attack us, we need to consider the big, obvious places but also the little, subtle ones.

The Evil One does not have power to destroy you. He cannot kill you or wrestle you away from God; by no means is he the counterpart of God in terms of power. Essentially, the single power he has is to tempt you. If any human being's soul is destroyed, including yours or mine, it will be through temptation. The temptation battle is the most important battle you will ever fight.

Questions 4–6

When people experience sexual temptation, what's prompting it? Very often, underneath the temptation is loneliness, boredom, self-pity, or resentment, maybe at a spouse. If that's the case, focusing only on the sexual issues, trying really hard to resist that temptation, won't work. As long as we just focus on the surface, we won't get to the root of the problem. The first step to resisting this temptation might not be a battle with misplaced sexual desire. It could be the need to reestablish joy in the marriage.

To the extent that you have authentic joy, temptation is driven away. Temptation is always the offer of the illusion of joy—never joy itself. The more authentic joy you experience, the less the deceptive illusion of pseudo-joy will be appealing to you.

The question becomes: What do you need to do to increase the joy factor in your life? What activities and relationships can you pursue that both honor God and bring authentic joy? Maybe it's being in nature or listening to music. It could be time with friends or various sporting ventures.

As you pray, "God, lead me not into temptation. Deliver me from the evil one," you also might need to pray, "God, help me be a joyful person. Help me to find those things that will fill me with joy."

Questions 7–8

If you try to handle temptation on your own, you will fall. You need to have somebody you can go to and say, "I want you to feel free to confront me when you're concerned about my behavior. I give you an open door." When you're tempted, severely tempted, you need someone to call. In twelve-step programs, they talk about a sponsor. A sponsor is available anytime, night or day. We all need someone like this.

Such power exists in community. You might need to pray, "God, I need a confidante in my life. Help me think about who that might be. Help me to understand the next step I need to take to deepen my relationship with that person until I know them well enough and can trust them deeply enough that I can share with them from my heart."

Questions 9–11

If you are facing a specific temptation, take time to identify a passage or two in the Bible that speaks to that temptation. Write down the passage on a card and keep it in your purse or wallet. Enter the passage into your PDA or put it on your mirror in the bathroom. Keep it in front of your eyes and heart. Commit it to memory. Meditate on it. Most study Bibles have a concordance to help you find passages on key words and topics. You can also buy a computer search program to help you find passages on whatever topic you need to study.

Get the Word of God deep in your heart and soul. Then, when the enemy comes to tempt you—and he will—be ready to say, "It is written!"

Session Six — Yours Is the Kingdom and the Power and the Glory
MATTHEW 6:9–13

Questions 1–3

In some Bible translations this closing portion of the Lord's Prayer is actually in a footnote because not all of the ancient manuscripts include it. However, many of the manuscripts do, and since the first century, followers of Jesus have used these words to end the prayer.

Questions 4–6

Acts 12 is the account of believers who asked for God's intervention—and got it! Acts 12 is also a tale of two cities, the story of two kings. One of them was King Herod (not the same one who tried to have Jesus killed as a baby), who had James, the brother of John, executed. When he discovered the political response to that execution was positive, he decided to have Peter executed as well. Herod had Peter arrested, imprisoned, and heavily guarded, intending to carry out the death sentence after the Passover.

But the church was praying! The writer, Luke, says they were not just praying, but earnestly praying. This wasn't a half-hearted afterthought. They were pouring out their hearts.

In the battle of kingdoms, prayer is a powerful weapon. God decided to deliver the imprisoned disciple. Now imagine being Peter. You're in prison waiting to die. You're sound asleep—and whack! You've heard of *Touched by an Angel*? Peter was whacked by an angel. It was one of those high-testosterone cherubim that came to Peter. "Get up!"

Peter followed the angel out of the prison, but had no idea what was really happening, thinking it must be a dream or vision.

In other words, Peter didn't believe that God's power was really at work even though he had been a witness to the resurrection and Pentecost. He was still learning about the amazing power of God . . . just like we are.

The next thing you know, Peter was free. What a clash of kingdoms! Herod made a declaration, imprisoned Peter, and posted sixteen armed guards. God sent one angel and Peter was freed. God wins! And shortly thereafter, Herod died. Another turtle had fallen. But God is still on his throne.

Questions 7–8

One writer paraphrases the end of this prayer with these words: "Because you are the one in charge, you have all the power. And the glory too is all yours forever, which is just the way we want it." He writes, "Just the way we want it." Not a bad paraphrase for "amen."

The most important thing we followers of Jesus will do all week long is to glorify God's name, to proclaim his goodness and greatness with all of our heart, soul, and strength. God is the most glorious and wonderful being in this universe. Jesus is the most glorious person who ever walked the face of this earth. Our Father is closer than the air we breathe. He is all around us. We need to learn to cry out, "May your name be treasured and loved. May people, beginning with me, come to really see and believe how truly good and wonderful you are."

Questions 9–10

We started our study of this great prayer with the opening line, "Our Father who is all around us, hallowed be your name. May your name be treasured."

Think about this: One day it will be! The Bible has a lot to say about this name. Luke tells us that the life of the man named Jesus was ended as it began, by a decree from Caesar—"Crucify him." Now Caesar didn't make this decree personally; it was made by one of his lower-level bureaucrats. But it was done in Caesar's name, by Caesar's soldiers, to protect Caesar's glory and his kingdom, through Caesar's power, because all rival kings must be killed.

Luke, the historian, tells us that when Jesus' life began, Caesar made a decree in Bethlehem. Jesus' life ended when Caesar made a decree at Calvary. But here's the question: Whose will was really being done? Was it really Caesar's at the end of the day? From a human perspective it might look like Caesar was on the throne, lifting his finger to command what would happen. But his throne was a throne of turtles.

The apostle Paul says that another king was really at work. King Jesus, the true king, chose Calvary. Jesus, being in his very nature God, humbled himself and was born in Bethlehem. He walked this earth, the most glorious life any human being ever lived, and became obedient in death, even death on the cross. But that's not the end of the story, or the end of the kingdom or the power or the glory. Therefore, God exalted him to the highest place and gave him the name that is above every name. The name that will one day be hallowed and before whose owner every knee will bow.

We value your thoughts about what you've just read.
Please share them with us. You'll find contact information in the back of this book.

WILLOW
Willow Creek Association

Willow Creek Association
Vision, Training, Resources for Prevailing Churches

This resource was created to serve you and to help you build a local church that prevails. It is just one of many ministry tools that are part of the Willow Creek Resources® line, published by the Willow Creek Association together with Zondervan.

The Willow Creek Association (WCA) was created in 1992 to serve a rapidly growing number of churches from across the denominational spectrum that are committed to helping unchurched people become fully devoted followers of Christ. Membership in the WCA now numbers over 12,000 Member Churches worldwide from more than ninety denominations.

The Willow Creek Association links like-minded Christian leaders with each other and with strategic vision, training, and resources in order to help them build prevailing churches designed to reach their redemptive potential. Here are some of the ways the WCA does that.

- **The Leadership Summit**—a once a year, two-and-a-half-day conference to envision and equip Christians with leadership gifts and responsibilities. Presented live at Willow Creek as well as via satellite broadcast to over 130 locations across North America, this event is designed to increase the leadership effectiveness of pastors, ministry staff, volunteer church leaders, and Christians in the marketplace.

- **Ministry-Specific Conferences** — throughout each year the WCA hosts a variety of conferences and training events — both at Willow Creek's main campus and offsite, across the U.S., and around the world — targeting church leaders and volunteers in ministry-specific areas such as: small groups, preaching and teaching, the arts, children, students, volunteers, stewardship, etc.

- **Willow Creek Resources®** — provides churches with trusted and field-tested ministry resources in such areas as leadership, evangelism, spiritual formation, spiritual gifts, small groups, stewardship, student ministry, children's ministry, the use of the arts — drama, media, contemporary music — and more.

- **WCA Member Benefits** — includes substantial discounts to WCA training events, a 20 percent discount on all Willow Creek Resources®, *Defining Moments* monthly audio journal for leaders, quarterly *Willow* magazine, access to a Members-Only section on WillowNet, monthly communications, and more. Member Churches also receive special discounts and premier services through WCA's growing number of ministry partners — Select Service Providers — and save an average of $500 annually depending on the level of engagement.

For specific information about WCA conferences, resources, membership, and other ministry services contact:

Willow Creek Association
P.O. Box 3188
Barrington, IL 60011-3188
Phone: 847-570-9812
Fax: 847-765-5046
www.willowcreek.com

Just Walk Across the Room Curriculum Kit

Simple Steps Pointing People to Faith

Bill Hybels with *Ashley Wiersma*

In *Just Walk Across the Room*, Bill Hybels brings personal evangelism into the twenty-first century with a natural and empowering approach modeled after Jesus himself. When Christ "walked" clear across the cosmos more than 2,000 years ago, he had no forced formulas and no memorized script; rather, he came armed only with an offer of redemption for people like us, many of whom were neck-deep in pain of their own making.

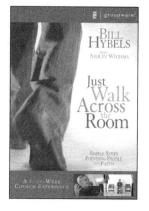

This dynamic four-week experience is designed to equip and inspire your entire church to participate in that same pattern of grace-giving by taking simple walks across rooms—leaving your circles of comfort and extending hands of care, compassion, and inclusiveness to people who might need a touch of God's love today.

Expanding on the principles set forth in Hybels' book of the same name, *Just Walk Across the Room* consists of three integrated components:

- Sermons, an implementation guide, and church promotional materials provided on CD-ROM to address the church as a whole
- Small group DVD and a participant's guide to enable people to work through the material in small, connected circles of community
- The book *Just Walk Across the Room* to allow participants to think through the concepts individually

Mixed Media Set: 978-0-310-27172-7

Pick up a copy at your favorite bookstore!

When the Game Is Over, It All Goes Back in the Box DVD

Six Sessions on Living Life in the Light of Eternity

John Ortberg with *Stephen* and *Amanda Sorenson*

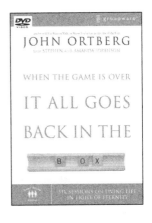

Using his humor and his genius for storytelling, John Ortberg helps you focus on the real rules of the game of life and how to set your priorities. *When the Game Is Over, It All Goes Back in the Box DVD* and participant's guide help explain how, left to our own devices, we tend to seek out worldly things, mistakenly thinking they will bring us fulfillment. But everything on Earth belongs to God. Everything we "own" is just on loan. And what pleases God is often 180 degrees from what we may think is important.

In the six sessions you will learn how to:

- Live passionately and boldly
- Learn how to be active players in the game that pleases God
- Find your true mission and offer your best
- Fill each square on the board with what matters most
- Seek the richness of being instead of the richness of having

You can't beat the house, notes Ortberg. We're playing our game of life on a giant board called a calendar. Time will always run out, so it's a good thing to live a life that delights your Creator. When everything goes back in the box, you'll have made what is temporary a servant to what is eternal, and you'll leave this life knowing you've achieved the only victory that matters.

This DVD includes a 32-page leader's guide and is designed to be used with the *When the Game Is Over, It All Goes Back in the Box* participant's guide, which is available separately.

DVD-ROM: 978-0-310-28247-1
Participant's Guide: 978-0-310-28246-4

Pick up a copy at your favorite bookstore!

The Case for Christ DVD

A Six-Session Investigation of the Evidence for Jesus

Lee Strobel and *Garry Poole*

Is there credible evidence that Jesus of Nazareth really is the Son of God?

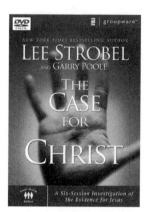

Retracing his own spiritual journey from atheism to faith, Lee Strobel, former legal editor of the *Chicago Tribune*, cross-examines several experts with doctorates from schools like Cambridge, Princeton, and Brandeis who are recognized authorities in their own fields.

Strobel challenges them with questions like:

- How reliable is the New Testament?
- Does evidence for Jesus exist outside the Bible?
- Is there any reason to believe the resurrection was an actual event?

Strobel's tough, point-blank questions make this six-session video study a captivating, fast-paced experience. But it's not fiction. It's a riveting quest for the truth about history's most compelling figure.

The six sessions include:

1. The Investigation of a Lifetime
2. Eyewitness Evidence
3. Evidence Outside the Bible
4. Analyzing Jesus
5. Evidence for the Resurrection
6. Reaching the Verdict

6 sessions; 1 DVD with leader's guide, 80 minutes (approximate).
The Case for Christ participant's guide is available separately.

DVD-ROM: 978-0-310-28280-8
Participant's Guide: 978-0-310-28282-2

The Case for a Creator DVD

A Six-Session Investigation of the Scientific Evidence That Points toward God

Lee Strobel and Garry Poole

Former journalist and skeptic Lee Strobel has discovered something very interesting about science. Far from being the enemy of faith, science may now provide a solid foundation for believing in God.

Has science finally discovered God? Certainly new discoveries in such scientific disciplines as cosmology, cellular biology, astronomy, physics and DNA research are pointing to the incredible complexity of our universe, a complexity best explained by the existence of a Creator.

Written by Lee Strobel and Garry Poole, this six-session, 80-minute DVD curriculum comes with a companion participant's guide along with a leader's guide. The kit is based on Strobel's book and documentary *The Case for a Creator* and invites participants to encounter a diverse and impressive body of new scientific research that supports the belief in God. Weighty and complex evidence is delivered in a compelling conversational style.

The six sessions include:

1. Science and God
2. Doubts about Darwinism
3. The Evidence of Cosmology
4. The Fine-tuning of the Universe
5. The Evidence of Biochemistry
6. DNA and the Origin of Life

The Case for a Creator participant's guide is available separately.

DVD-ROM: 978-0-310-28283-9
Participant's Guide: 978-0-310-28285-

The Case for Faith DVD

A Six-Session Investigation of the Toughest Objections to Christianity

Lee Strobel and *Garry Poole*

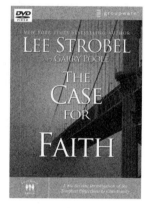

Doubt is familiar territory for Lee Strobel, the former atheist and award-winning author of books for skeptics and Christians. But he believes that faith and reason go hand in hand, and that Christianity is a defensible religion.

In this six-session video curriculum, Strobel uses his journalistic approach to explore the most common emotional obstacles to faith in Christ. These include the natural inclination to wrestle with faith and doubt, the troubling presence of evil and suffering in the world, and the exclusivity of the Christian gospel. They also include this compelling question: Can I doubt and be a Christian?

Through compelling video of personal stories and experts addressing these topics, combined with reflection and interaction, Christians and spiritual seekers will learn how to overcome these obstacles, deepen their spiritual convictions, and find new confidence that Christianity is a reasonable faith.

The Case for Faith participant's guide is available separately.

DVD-ROM: 978-0-310-24116-4
Participant's Guide: 978-0-310-24114-0

Pick up a copy at your favorite bookstore!

ZONDERVAN®
.com

ReGroup™

Training Groups to Be Groups

Henry Cloud, Bill Donahue, and *John Townsend*

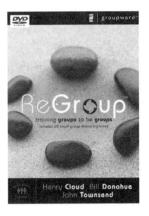

Whether you're a new or seasoned group leader, or whether your group is well-established or just getting started, the *ReGroup™* small group DVD and participant's guide will lead you and your group together to a remarkable new closeness and effectiveness. Designed to foster healthy group interaction and facilitate maximum growth, this innovative approach equips both group leaders and members with essential skills and values for creating and sustaining truly life-changing small groups. Created by three group life experts, the two DVDs in this kit include:

- Four sixty-minute sessions on the foundations of small groups that include teaching by the authors, creative segments, and activities and discussion time
- Thirteen five-minute coaching segments on topics such as active listening, personal sharing, giving and receiving feedback, prayer, calling out the best in others, and more

A participant's guide is sold separately.

DVD: 978-0-310-27783-5
Participant's Guide: 978-0-310-27785-9

Pick up a copy at your favorite bookstore!

No Perfect People Allowed (with 4-Week Church Experience DVD)

Creating a Come as You Are Culture in the Church

John Burke

How do we live out the message of Jesus in today's ever-changing culture?

The church is facing its greatest challenge—and its greatest opportunity—in our postmodern, post-Christian world. God is drawing thousands of spiritually curious "imperfect people" to become his church—but how are we doing at welcoming them?

No Perfect People Allowed shows you how to deconstruct the five main barriers standing between emerging generations and your church by creating the right culture. From inspiring stories of real people once far from God, to practical ideas that can be applied by any local church, this book offers a refreshing vision of the potential and power of the body of Christ to transform lives today.

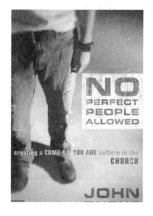

"We now are living in a post-Christian America—and that means we must be rethinking ministry through a missionary mindset. What makes this book both unique and extremely helpful is that it is filled with real-life stories of post-Christian people becoming followers of Jesus—not just statistics or data about them."

Dan Kimball, Author, *The Emerging Church*

"...John's 'get it' factor with people, lost or found, is something to behold! Reading this book filled me with optimism regarding the next generation of pastors and faith communities..."

Bill Hybels, Senior Pastor, Willow Creek Community Church

"*No Perfect People Allowed* is a timely and necessary word for church leaders in a post-Christian culture. John Burke serves up quite a tasty meal full of the rich nutrients that will strengthen the body of Christ."

Randy Frazee, Senior Minister, Oak Hills Church;
Author, *The Connecting Church* and *Making Room for Life*

Hardcover, Jacketed: 978-0-310-27807-8

Share Your Thoughts

With the Author: Your comments will be forwarded to
the author when you send them to *zauthor@zondervan.com.*

With Zondervan: Submit your review of this book
by writing to *zreview@zondervan.com.*

Free Online Resources at
www.zondervan.com/hello

 Zondervan AuthorTracker: Be notified whenever your
favorite authors publish new books, go on tour, or post
an update about what's happening in their lives.

 Daily Bible Verses and Devotions: Enrich your life
with daily Bible verses or devotions that help you start
every morning focused on God.

 Free Email Publications: Sign up for newsletters on
fiction, Christian living, church ministry, parenting, and
more.

 Zondervan Bible Search: Find and compare
Bible passages in a variety of translations at
www.zondervanbiblesearch.com.

 Other Benefits: Register yourself to receive online
benefits like coupons and special offers, or to participate
in research.